The Country Life Picture Book of Scotland

The Country Life Picture Book of
Scotland

Lord Tweedsmuir

Photography by
W. F. Davidson and R. Thomlinson

COUNTRY LIFE BOOKS

frontispiece
Loch Tulla, near Bridge of Orchy

Published by Country Life Books,
an imprint of The Hamlyn Publishing Group Limited
Michelin House, 81 Fulham Road
London SW3 6RB
and distributed for them by
Octopus Distribution Services Limited
Rushden, Northamptonshire, England NN10 9RZ.

First published 1977
Sixth impression 1988

ISBN 0 600 38250 8

Printed by Mandarin Offset, Hong Kong

Scotland
A personal view

This book gathers together more than a hundred pictures of Scotland. In sunlight and shadow. In winter and summer. It is pictures like these that wandering Scots carry in their minds as they seek their fortunes all over the world and their thoughts turn back to Scotland. We love Scotland, but we wander. Scotland is our home. But the world is our opportunity. Those who leave Scotland to seek their fortunes have powerful gifts to offer. One of them is a genius for survival, which is not an art, or a science, and least of all is it an accident. We can go to the ends of the earth and live there perfectly happily. We see the globe with reference to the home in which we grew up. A wounded Jock, in a military hospital in the First World War, was asked where he had got his wound, and replied: 'Twa miles on the Rothiemurchus side of Baghdad.' Few would deny that we are the most powerful small race since the ancient Greeks, because we have regarded the world as our own parish, and have settled all over it. And the world is, on the whole, very tolerant of us. Many of those who wander return to their homes to retire. I remember spending my boyhood summer holidays at Peebles, and my uncle, who lived there, told me of seeing a man leaning over Tweed bridge, obviously in a great state of concern. As he drew nearer he heard him say, 'I tell't them that the Tweed at Peebles was jist twice as wide as the Hooghly at Calcutta, and I tell't a muckle lee.'

We tend to seek our fortunes abroad for more than one reason. One of them is that we have a strong rule of primogeniture. A farmer's six sons help him on the farm, and when he dies the eldest gets the farm, and the others have to go and seek their fortunes. And our native gifts sell higher the further that we travel. And secondly, our famous universities, of which we used to have only four and now have many others, produce far more highly educated people than those for whom there can ever be highly educated jobs. In Aberdeen we had two universities in the days when the whole of England had only two. If you look at the beautiful tower of King's College, surmounted by its stone crown, you will realise that we are a Continental people. The stone crown on that tower is the crown of the Holy Roman Empire. It was put there when Lorenzo the Magnificent reigned in Florence, and we were part of the great European Renaissance, a part which perished in one ghastly rainy afternoon at the Battle of Flodden, at the beginning of the 16th century. Thereafter nearly a hundred years passed when we were so impoverished that it was said there was only one painter in Scotland who got more than twice for the painting what the carpenter got for making the frame. Then in the century following came our second renaissance. Art and science burgeoned, and the revenue rose 52 times largely because, since the Act of the Union of the two crowns in 1707, we were now allowed to trade with what had, until then, been English colonies. And as those colonies expanded, and what was then called the Empire expanded with them, so Scotland expanded most mightily.

You can see the Continental influence in the office of Rector in our universities, which is an entirely Continental concept. It is the Continental concept of a students' democracy where the students can, by their own franchise, elect their own man who is a match in power for the head of the University. You can see it in our architecture: there are old castles which resemble many French and Flemish castles. You can see that they grew up at the same time, and with the same way of thinking in architecture. You can see it in the old crow-stepped gabled houses in Edinburgh and a hundred other places, reminiscent of the ones you see in old Dutch masters. We had strong ties with Holland in those days – the Scots Brigade in the Dutch army were as good troops as you could find in Europe. The valley of the Don in Aberdeenshire is sometimes called the Scottish Loire, for the number of castles there.

Certainly if you take the catchment area of the Don, and add the catchment of the Dee, you will find them in plenty, and you can trace the influence of half a dozen other European countries in their building. Not all the castles that you see are ruined merely by age. Many were knocked down by the Kings' direct order when they housed powerful and unruly barons. After Cromwell won the battle of Dunbar he had the great fortresses of Dunbar and Tantallon and Dirleton all 'dinged doon', as we say. There is a little pele tower on the upper Tweed which is now a few moss-grown rocks and slabs of stone. One of the early Kings thought he would travel his kingdom incognito to find out what his people thought, and on passing this castle he was set upon by the owner of it and robbed of absolutely everything he owned. He came back with an army, and those slabs of stone you see from the hillside have lain there ever since, gathering moss.

We are divided in most people's thinking, and in all reality, into the Highlands and the Lowlands with a central belt in the middle. Many think of the Highlands in terms of high latitude when it really means high country, high mountains. In fact there is a region called the North-east Lowlands which runs north along the coast from Aberdeen and turns right back into the Moray Firth and up to Inverness following the seashore. It is a belt of low-lying farmland, which in all conscience is far north, because Aberdeen itself is 100 miles further north than Moscow. The phrase 'the Highland line' conveys to many something like a line of latitude drawn across the middle of Scotland, but in fact the Highlands reach down, on the west coast, almost to Glasgow itself. In that way, the Highland line is like the Arctic Circle which, although shown as a straight line round the globe, cuts the Greenland ice-cap in half; and they pasture cattle to the north of it in Scandinavia, while true arctic conditions extend in Canada south to the bottom of Hudson's Bay, several hundred miles below this imaginary

line. When you clear the Scottish mainland to the north you are in country which owes nothing to the Celt, but has its origins with, and owed its allegiance to, the Norsemen. The northermost island of Shetland is crowned by a lighthouse, on the same latitude as southern Greenland.

Scotland has a marked difference not only between her sons of the Highlands and the Lowlands but between those of the East and the West as well. At our 'first footing' ceremonies on New Year's Eve it is unlucky in the east to have a fairhaired man cross your threshhold, because it might once have been a Norse invader. By the same token, a dark-haired man is unlucky in the west, as he might have been a pirate from one of the western European coasts.

It is not surprising that the early history of England and Scotland was one of enmity, as there were two versions of all historical events in which they were jointly involved. Things look exactly different from different sides of a border. One of Scotland's most famous warriors, the Black Douglas, commanded the Scottish left at Bannockburn and was knighted on that battlefield. He was a figure of terror south of the border. Mothers on the English side crooned to their children a little couplet that runs:

'Hush ye, hush ye,
Little pet, ye,
Hush ye, hush ye,
Do not fret ye.
The Black Douglas,
Shall not get ye.'

But to us in Scotland the Black Douglas was a model of propriety – 'the Good Lord James' we called him. We live very close to history in Scotland; it is always within easy reach and not only in Scotland, for we find our own footprints all over the world. I often pause in Westminster Hall to look at the brass plaque which shows the step in the Hall upon which William Wallace, the great patriot, stood at his trial there on 22nd August 1305.

The Highlands and the Lowlands had long historic quarrels until the 14th century when a battle called the Red Harlaw settled for ever that the north of Scotland was not going to run the south.

I heard, not long ago, two members of the media discussing where the true spirit of Scotland really lay. And they came to the conclusion that it could be found probably at its strongest on the football terraces and in the housing estates. Where such a substantial number of the Scots, in fact several millions of them, are to be found, a very great deal of the spirit of Scotland must be found there too. But the spirit of Scotland is a many-sided thing, and the spirit of all the Scots all over the world, and of their descendants, contributes to it. It is strong in the hearts that beat under Scottish uniforms. It is where smoke rises from a dwelling in the glens and the farmlands. It is where the fisher-folk and the oilrig men face the endless procession of the waves. It is where clocks in tall towers scatter their chimes over places of learning and centres of commerce.

The Scottish crofter is something that is very specially Scottish. People see the tiny farmhouse, and the tiny plots of land, and assume that they are looking at people whose poverty is such that they are almost destitute. They are greatly mistaken. The Scottish crofter is a proud man and very much his own man. His way of life is recognised; he has rights enshrined in rules and regulations watched over by the Crofters' Commission. Nowadays it is common to find a crofter living on one croft and working a second croft together with his own, and making a pretty satisfactory living out of it. They are splendidly independent people. An earlier Secretary of State for Scotland told me that he hit on the idea of giving a plough free to a certain number of crofters to see if they could not be spurred on to tilling the ground, to a greater degree than they were doing at the time. That summer he went to the Hebrides to look after various things,

but particularly to see what they had done with his ploughs. He was taken to a croft to which one of his ploughs had been delivered. There it was beside the road, almost invisible under the grass and the nettles. So he asked his Gaelic interpreter to speak to the crofter and ask him: 'Why have you not used your plough?' The interpreter with a great deal of gesture, and in that wonderful rise and fall of the Gaelic tongue, talked away for about ten minutes. He then turned to my friend with a sort of inner serenity on his face: 'The man says he has no inclination to use his plough.'

This part of Scotland is the focus of the thoughts of very many generations of Scottish emigrants to Canada, America, New Zealand, Australia and all the world over. That lovely poem 'The Canadian Boat Song' carries these marvellous words:

From the lone shieling of the misty island
Mountains divide us, and the waste of seas,
Yet still the blood is strong, the heart is Highland,
And we in dreams behold the Hebrides.

This is the country of the Gaelic speaker.

When I first went to Canada forty years ago there were more sermons in Gaelic in Cape Breton Island, in Nova Scotia, than there were in the whole of Scotland. The Highland Clearances at the end of the 18th century and during much of the 19th brought about a massive depopulation which would clearly have happened anyhow, before many more years had passed. There is a beautiful tributary of the upper Dee, the River Ey, whose valley once held a large population that walked down the glen to the church every Sabbath in their Sunday best. They lived off raising tough, short-legged cattle which they drove over the mountains periodically, to the cattle trysts. For the rest, they made whisky, and you can still see the funnel-shaped pits in which they distilled it. It sold for a very good price outside. This last was not only to circumvent the law, which it did, but to provide them with a staple industry. As far as I know, nobody ever cleared

Caledonian Canal at Corpach, near Fort William.

them off the land. They disappeared because their way of life simply became untenable in a changing world.

Scotland's long indented sea-coast has had an inevitable effect on its sons. It is a tremendous nursery for fishermen and seamen of all kinds. The Lord Provost of Aberdeen, whose office is about 700 years old, is ex-officio a Vice-Admiral of the Shores of Great Britain and Ireland. Round this coast battered Armada galleons in 1588 tottered their way back to Spain. One of them sank in the bay at Tobermory, and part of it has been recovered. Another sank close to where I live in Aberdeenshire; the crew scrambled ashore and were well treated by the local inhabitants, which was

very unusual in those days. They were called 'Philip's men' after King Philip of Spain, and there are many people called Philips there to this day, who are said to look slightly different from all the rest. Before the big deep-sea trawlers came, all the fishing was done from the fishing villages with a tiny mole to guard the little harbour that sheltered them from storms.

The coming of the deep-sea trawler vastly extended the range of the fishermen, although Aberdeen trawlers relatively rarely go to Iceland or the distant waters. They mostly fish round the Faeroe Islands and leave the faraway grounds to the men of Hull and Grimsby. Aberdeen itself is the third biggest fishing port in Britain, having once been a very prosperous whaling port, before the invention of gas killed the market for whale-oil. When I was a boy about fifty years ago there was still a whaling station in use in the island of Harris in the Hebrides. The deep-sea fishermen have a world of their own, apart from ordinary men. They see their wives on average about once every seven days in the year. If you listen to the shipping forecast, you will hear intoned those evocative names, 'Iceland, Faeroes, Fair Isle, Bailey, Hebrides, Rockall', and picture the masthead lights rising and falling in the long cold seas.

A new frontier has been added to Scotland. A new element has come into our lives with the oil discoveries. Aberdeen harbour has been considerably enlarged and contains the most extraordinary-looking vessels, all to do with oilrigs. Every day twenty or thirty helicopters fly over the city headed for a hundred and some miles out to sea. There are now two American schools and one French school in Aberdeen for the use of the oil-drilling fraternity who come from those parts, and no one is in the least surprised to see men wearing a Stetson hat in any part of Aberdeen.

Some people tell us that we have reached a time when a millennium of perpetual prosperity is with us, arising from the oil. But we have a long history in Scotland, and we tend to be very sceptical of talk like this. We always say we will believe it when we see it.

Intensely wild as much of Scotland is, a great deal can be seen from the roads themselves. The Highland roads, with their passing places at intervals, call for a special technique of driving. You must judge whether you or the oncoming car is closer to the passing place, and whichever is the nearer draws in there. A fine code of politeness flowers from touching your hat to the other man if he has accommodated you in this way. Marshal Wade was sent to build roads in the Highlands so that armies could get in there and if necessary keep

the clans in order. When the 1745 Rebellion came, the rebellious Highlanders used the good Marshal's roads for themselves to speed their march south. The difference between Highlands and Lowlands is one that you can feel immediately. It is a way of life and a separate people.

In the borders of Scotland the sheep play a very great part, and the woollen mills all down the Tweed handle the harvest of the flocks from the hills all round them. Although there are many sheep in the Highlands, the real sheep country is the Borders. I remember so well as a boy the great flocks of sheep, some of which still followed the green drove roads over the hills, while others were driven along highways followed by almost apoplectic motorists, who had to go at the pace of the sheep that they found themselves behind. When the flock was coming the other way, the motorist merely halted while the woolly flood eddied round him. On the tombstones of many Lowland churchyards you can read the inscriptions to the memory of shepherds who have perished in the many great snowstorms. They still do so. Often the inscription says that the shepherd's dog stayed with his master and perished with him. A shepherd's dog does nothing except on orders. If his master cannot give him orders he will not move. It is said that a collie will do five times the distance his master does, when they are rounding up sheep, and as it is nothing for his master to walk sixteen miles in a day, his dog may be covering round about eighty. I remember as a little boy being taken to the old kirk at the village of Tweedsmuir, and watching fascinated the shepherds sitting in rows, their collie-dogs lying under the pews, while their masters wrestled in prayer.

You never lose that recollection of the sheep crying on the hills on the other side of the glen, and following an unseen path like a string of irregular pearls, while you watch the cloud-shadows chase each other across those hillsides. These are hills that Robert Louis Stevenson described in wonderful words: 'Here the wind blows as it blows in the ship's rigging, hard and cold and pure, and the hilltops huddle together, one behind another, like cattle into the sunset.'

Visitors from England are often struck by the absence of little old village churches which are so much a part of the English countryside. For the Scottish village church was in a poorer and much less populated country and was always of a simpler construction. Many were replaced in the late 19th century by some large steepled edifice. The standing stones go back a long way to the time when man kept no record of anything that remains to us. They were reared up to worship some god no man knows who. Since then the Kirk of Scotland has been the centre of so much turbulence, culminating in the Reformation. The reformer John Knox was no friend to art and beauty and literature. Many of the great abbeys and cathedrals perished, to add to those that had been reduced to ruins in Scotland's earlier wars of independence. The citizens of Edinburgh steadfastly defended their own St Giles' cathedral from the zeal of the Reformers who would have smashed its beautiful glass and woodwork. Happily in Aberdeen, having done this very thing to our St Machar's cathedral, they overlooked the beautiful university chapel of King's College which remains as a gem for ever. The tiny Hebridean island of Iona holds the simple tombs of the old kings of Scotland who were taken there for burial.

The Lowlands never had the same clan system as the Highlands. Many people wonder how it worked. It was an interesting system of government where one clan owned an area of land in common, and followed their clan leader to battle, who in turn protected them as best he could. When the clan had to turn out for war, they went through the seniors of the clan until they found a man entirely adequate for the job. An example is provided by the Farquharsons on upper Deeside, on whose lands you can still see the great Scots pines of the Caledonian

forest. When the fiery cross went round to gather the clans for Prince Charlie's landing in 1745 they looked to their own battleline. The leader of the clan was a hopeless invalid, the next in line was suspected of pro-Government sympathies, the next was a seasoned soldier who had fought in the foreign wars on the Continent, and he it was who led the clan into battle until he was badly wounded at Falkirk. For the last round of the tragedy at Culloden, the Clan of the Cat was led by a certain Farquharson of Monaltrie (Bonnie Monaltrie of the Golden Hair), and it clawed deep into the battle line of Cumberland's army. Monaltrie was imprisoned in the Tower, and had his writing-desk sent all the way down to him on a cart so that he could write his letters in peace. He was finally pardoned and returned to his glen again to find that a new Scotland had been born.

And then there is that middle part, often called by that sadly dull name, 'the Central Belt'. It is the scene of much Scottish history and of most of Scotland's heavy industry. Here you will find the scenes of some of our greatest memories. At Stirling, William Wallace defeated the English, and at Bannockburn, nearby, Robert the Bruce won the war of independence which he had fought for most of his life. At Falkirk, Wallace was defeated and never re-established his army. The tired Highlanders following Prince Charlie back in his retreat from Derby managed to fight off the Government forces there, and put off for a little the inevitable defeat that was to come at Culloden.

Edinburgh is old. But so is Glasgow, whose university is well into its sixth century of existence. At the end of the 18th century, Glasgow lost one immensely valuable industry and gained many others. As the century came to an end heavier grew the pall of smoke as Glasgow's industry expanded. But with the war against George Washington's America, they lost their immensely valuable tobacco trade which they had enjoyed for so long. They say in Glasgow: 'God made the country, but man made the Clyde.' And certainly the Clyde is a triumphant conversion of a not very large river into one of the great ship-building ports of the world. Long after I have forgotten everything else, I shall remember the sight of the QE2 riding down her slipway with a clanking of chains and a churning of muddy waters; launched into history.

The 18th century was Scotland's century. The Union of the two crowns in 1707 was hotly discussed then and is still discussed now. The benefits of it were slow in coming because we had two wars, in the 1715 and 1745 rebellions. In the second half of the century things began to move, and art and science, architecture and commerce blossomed. The Union added a completely new dimension to life, which was slowly becoming more comfortable. Houses, it was true, were mostly built without any window on the cold north side. Nearly all of them had herb gardens to try to disguise the appalling smells of living, and also to give some flavour to the wretched diet of salted meat put down every autumn to last through the whole winter. Now, however, new architects, like the Adam brothers, were putting up some of the most graceful houses in the whole of Britain. But few yet wanted to go to Scotland – as a result of the two wars and long-inherited hatred, Scotland was disliked heartily on the south side of the border. As the Scots loathed the English, the English despised the Scots, and were incapable of seeing that Scotland was beautiful. The lovely Drumlanrig Castle, in Dumfriesshire, was described by one English visitor (Englishmen only visited Scotland if they absolutely had to for some business reason) as looking like 'a beautiful picture in a dirty grotto'. The describer went on to talk about the hideousness of the hills. Dr Johnson on his Scottish tours expressed the English view on Scotland very tersely. He wrote in his diary comments about it which might have been appropriate to a 19th-century explorer talking about darkest Africa. They

all talked about the absence of inns, the treeless wastes and much else in the same vein. But the world was to change fast in that century. The clansmen who had fought with Prince Charlie at Culloden were to be found fighting in the British army in 1759 at the capture of Quebec. They left their mark there too. They were there for the whole of the first winter through some aberration of officialdom and, because they were used to curling with stones at home, they filled copper kettles with water, froze them and used them for curling. This is why for many years Canadians used irons for curling and not curling-stones. They were logging the forests on the upper Spey and upper Dee to fuel the rapidly growing industries of the Central Belt. But it still needed a catalyst to make people really understand Scotland.

And it came with that quiet man, Sir Walter Scott, a great and kindly genius, whose wonderful romantic nature gave the world an entirely new feeling about Scotland. Quite suddenly, everyone saw it as beautiful and romantic and very much alive. He put new heart into an old land, and for the first time the Scots found themselves welcoming appreciative visitors from all over the world, and being welcome there themselves.

If I might venture to advise a visitor to Scotland, do not try to see too much at one time. The variety is infinite, and its other charms will keep for another day.

Glen Sligachan, Skye, one of the great rock climbs of the world.

A 'black house', or crofter's cottage, at Kilmuir, Skye (right). Flora Macdonald was buried in the graveyard here in 1790, and the Celtic cross marking her grave carries an inscription by Dr Johnson. Crofters' cottages are common in the more remote parts of Scotland, but none is better preserved than the one at Luib, near Broadford, Skye (below right). It is often difficult to imagine how crofters could make a living from anything except sheep, but with hard work respectable harvests are possible, as can be seen at Staffin, Skye (below).

Ben Storr (2,360ft) and the 160ft pinnacle of the
'Old Man of Storr' (right) are, with Loch Fada,
familiar features of the Trotternish landscape on Skye.
As always there are the roadside sheep.

*The contrast between the crofter's cottage at
Bornaritaig, Camas Mor (above), and Dunvegan
Castle (left), Skye, is proof, to 20th-century eyes, of
the huge gap that existed between a great clan chief
and his people. But this ignores the mutual obligations
imposed by the clan system on the chiefs, who, if they
often lived better than other men, had also to provide
protection for their own people. Not all chiefs were as
rich and powerful as the Macleod of Macleod, whose
seat is still Dunvegan Castle, a rallying for Macleods
from all over the world.*

*From the pier at Uig, Skye, the ferry prepares to
leave for North Uist and Harris* (below).

*Turning the first furrow on virgin land at Claigan,
Skye* (bottom).

Blaven, Skye (below right).

Sgurr nan Gillean (3,167ft) looms over Glen Sligachan in the Cuillins, Skye (below). *By contrast, only the lack of palm trees prevents one mistaking the golden sands of Tolsta Head* (top right), *on the island of Lewis, for the West Indies.*

Remote in both time and space, the group of standing stones at Callanish (bottom), in a lonely corner of the island of Lewis, is second in importance only to Stonehenge. A circle of thirteen monoliths is surrounded by rows of other stones radiating outwards and including a clear avenue. The orientation of the group makes it likely that prehistoric man used the stones to determine the equinoxes, the summer solstice and other important dates in primitive agriculture.

All over Europe the fishing industry is, as always, in a period of reappraisal. The inshore fishing boats at Kyleakin (right), Skye, look prosperous, but on the east coast, at Aberdeen (above), Scotland's largest fishing port, the vessels must brave the long cold seas of the north.

The Storr (below) *and Bioda Buidhe and Ben Edra
seen from the Quiraing* (left), *on the island of Skye,
provide some of the most fantastic and unearthly
landscapes in Scotland.*

Skye has some of the most varied and spectacular scenery in the whole of Scotland. These views of Blaven and Loch Slapin (left) and the strange rock pinnacles of Storr (above) would be hard to match in any country. One is tempted to seek parallels between such rugged uncompromising landscapes and the Scottish character. But this is a half-truth. The people of the Highlands and Islands are gentle, patient and courteous, like countrypeople everywhere, though they are rugged as well.

Much of the work in sheepfarming, rounding-up and shearing, for instance, is organised on a communal basis on Lewis (opposite page).

Duntulm Castle (below), *Skye, was once the stronghold of the Macdonalds of the Isles.*

At Broadford Bay (above), *Skye, the sun comes up over the Scottish mainland, while further down the coast, at Kyleakin, Castle Moil* (left) *guards the approach to the island from across the narrows.*

From Spean Bridge.

Glen Coe (opposite page), *scene of one of the grimmest incidents in Scottish history, has an atmosphere that anyone can feel even on the brightest day. It was from Signal Rock, where the piper stands* (right), *that in a cold February dawn of 1692 the signal was given which started the Campbell soldiers hunting their Macdonald hosts through the houses and up into the hills where many survivors of the slaughter were to die of exposure. In Gaelic, Glen Coe means 'Glen of Weeping'. The Three Sisters, shown in this view* (below) *from the old road, rise to between 2,500 and 3,000ft high.*

The River Glenbeg (above) *is famous for salmon and trout.*

This area of Rothiemurchus Forest (left) *has such poor soil, consisting as it does of glacial sands and gravels, that it can support only those hardy pine and birch, with some juniper – and of course the heather.*

*Loch Ness, home of the 'monster', whose fans keep a
hopeful watch (top right), is one of the lochs in the
Great Glen. The Caledonian Canal, seen here (bottom
right) where it runs into Loch Ness, turns this chain
of lochs into a busy waterway. But the old Ballachulish
ferry (below), between Fort William and Glen Coe,
has now been replaced by a bridge.*

The opposing pressures of tourism and conservation are sometimes hard to reconcile. But apparently secluded Achmelvich Bay (bottom right) has succeeded. There is a skilfully concealed caravan site here. Indeed, for the tourist there is much of absorbing interest in the varied coastline, from the deeply etched rocks of Clashnessie Bay (top right), Sutherland, to beautiful Gruinard Bay (below), Ross and Cromarty, where the 'raised beaches' show how the relative heights of sea and land have changed at different times.

This Pictish broch (above) is one of the best-preserved
that has come down to us. Unique to Scotland, these
massive towers were made without mortar, much like
a dry-stone wall, and consisted of a series of chambers
in the thickness of the outer wall, all opening on to a
central court open to the sky. The scale is huge. The
inner court may be as much as 50 feet across.

Peaceful Loch an Eilean (left), in Rothiemurchus
Forest, once harboured the notorious Wolf of
Badenoch, the ruins of whose stronghold, the Castle of
the Comyns, still stand on an island in the loch. For
many years an osprey nested here.

The gardens of Inverewe House (top right) *are one of the most unexpected sights in the northwestern Highlands. Semi-tropical trees and plants have been flourishing here on the same latitude as Hudson's Bay and the steppes of Siberia. Yet just over a century ago this promontory, lapped by the Gulf Stream, was no different from the rest of this coast — rocky and barren of all except heather. It is a remarkable oasis in a damp desert. In other parts of Scotland, as at Highland Cottage, Coylumbridge* (bottom right), *Inverness-shire, gardening is simpler.*

Loch Dubh (below), *between Loch Eil and Glenfinnan, on the Road to the Isles.*

Loch Rannoch and Schiehallion (the other side of Schiehallion can be seen on pages 80–81).

Eilean Donan Castle (left), at the point where Loch Alsh meets Loch Duich, was bombarded by a British warship during a Jacobite rising in 1719, before the present causeway was built. It was to commemorate a conflict with more far-reaching consequences than this that the cairn (above) was built on the battlefield of Culloden.

(Below) *Plockton's livelihood has changed over the last few decades. The traditional fishing and crofting have gradually declined and are being replaced by newer occupations, such as tourism and forestry. Plockton's fine sheltered anchorage makes it a favourite base for yachtsmen, while the continual improvement in the network of roads brings more visitors every year to these small communities. One of the traditional crafts that has benefited from the tourist trade is weaving—this loom (top right) is in Inverness—while a totally new form of agriculture, fish farming, seen here (bottom right) at Loch Ailort, is beginning to make an impact.*

Away from the north and west, the land becomes noticeably gentler and more pastoral: at Dornoch Firth (bottom left), *Sutherland, farming seems to the outsider to be less of a struggle than in the west. Industry, on the other hand, can flourish in the Highlands, where its constructions often seem to take on something of the grandeur of the landscape. Both the hydroelectric dam at Loch Laggan* (below) *and the pulp mill at Fort William* (top left) *make use of natural resources, water and timber, abundantly available in the Highlands.*

The Five Sisters (below), *rising to over 3,500ft,*
dominate Loch Duich.

The summit plateau of Cairn Gorm (above), at above 4,000ft, presents one of the bleakest views imaginable, a fact which the ptarmigan relies on to provide the solitude necessary for untroubled nesting (top). It is hard to realise that the Cairngorms are only the core of a vast mountain range of over 20,000ft which has during vast stretches of geological time worn down to its present height.

In autumn the deer-grass lends additional colour to this view (above) of the Ben Nevis group from Glen Spean.

Highland cattle on a narrow road by Loch Quoich are a reminder to motorists that roads are not merely for their use.

Salen, on Loch Sunart, Argyllshire.

Elgin Cathedral (above) *has suffered more misfortunes than most, ranging from its sacking by the Wolf of Badenoch in 1390 to the fall of the central tower in 1711, after which the 'Lantern of the North' became for a hundred years just a source of building material for the neighbourhood. However, the west portal is among the surviving parts.*

Doune Castle (left), *Perthshire, dates from the early 15th century. It was held for the Prince in 1745.*

The Falls of Killin, on the River Dochart.

Near Auldearn (above), *Nairn, Montrose routed the Covenanters in 1645.*

Ben Lawers (right), *on the northwest side of Loch Tay, is famous for its rare wild flowers, as well as for its beauty.*

Rest and Be Thankful, 900ft up between Loch Long and Loch Fyne.

St Columba spent 34 years in Iona, where he arrived from Ireland in 563, and the quiet island has ever since attracted pilgrims. The Cathedral (below), dating mainly from the 15th or 16th century, and the monastic buildings attached have been considerably restored in the present century, after a long history of successive destruction and rebuilding.

St Conan's Kirk (right), *Loch Awe, stands at the opposite historical extreme: this church, not far from Oban where the visitor to Iona arrives back on the mainland was dedicated in its present form in 1930.*

Carrick Castle (left) *stands at the end of a narrow road along the shore of Loch Goil, as remote a site as it is possible to imagine for a man's house. But the Earls of Argyll evidently felt the need to dominate the countryside for one of them built the castle in the 14th century. It is symptomatic of the turbulent history of Scotland that such strongholds were needed in the Highlands until relatively recent times. Bernera Barracks* (above), *for instance, on the north side of Glenelg Bay, was built after the abortive rebellion of 1719, and was garrisoned by troops until the 1790s. Castle Carrick did not survive so long: it was burnt in 1685.*

*The Forest of Mamlorn, Perthshire, shows itself in
different colours according to the season.*

It is extraordinary that such an apparently impregnable fortress as Stirling Castle (left) should ever have been captured, but Wallace in 1297, Edward I in 1304 and General Monk in 1651 all managed that feat, although Prince Charles Edward, perhaps characteristically, failed in 1746.

A few miles from Stirling stands the monument to Robert the Bruce (above) on the famous battlefield of Bannockburn, where the background of seemingly incongruous modern houses reminds us that the Scots always have the air of living their lives in, among, and totally involved with, their history.

The Oban fisherman's work does not stop when his boat is in port. Gear must be checked and nets mended. But across the harbour there is leisure for some.

Between Blair Atholl and Pitlochry the wooded River Garry (above) runs peacefully through the pass of Killiecrankie where, in 1689, General Mackay was defeated by the Highlanders under Graham of Claverhouse, Viscount Dundee (Scott's 'Bonnie Dundee'). Close by is another quiet view (left) across Loch Tummel to Schiehallion (also to be seen on pages 48–49).

The fishing fleet at Pittenweem, Fife.

The striking colour of St Abb's Head (below) *is due
to the Lower Old Red Sandstone.*

*Sir Walter Scott and Field-Marshal Earl Haig are
both buried in Dryburgh Abbey* (bottom right),
*Berwickshire. Founded in 1150 by monks from across
the border at Alnwick, the Abbey was ironically right
in the path of English forces coming up from the south
and was several times severely damaged in consequence.
Occupation Lane* (top right), *dappled by the autumn
sun, may be an echo of those troubled times.*

*Close to Dryburgh are two more Abbeys, Jedburgh
and Melrose. Jedburgh* (right), *founded early in the
12th century, is built of red sandstone and, though
like Dryburgh much damaged, still stands impressively
beside the Jed Water. The Cistercian Melrose Abbey*
(above), *founded in 1136 by monks from the Yorkshire
Abbey of Rievaulx, has flying buttresses and other
architectural features more common south of the border.
In summer many visitors are attracted to the superbly
kept gardens* (top).

The 17th-century Preston Mill (above), near East Linton, East Lothian, is maintained in working order by the National Trust for Scotland.

Neidpath Castle (left), just outside Peebles, was built by the Frasers in the 15th century. This stronghold par excellence, with its 11ft-thick walls, was forced to surrender to Cromwell.

Baled straw after the harvest near Eckford, in Teviotdale.

(Left) *A 20th-century shepherd and his dog pause by the statue of the poet James Hogg, the 'Ettrick Shepherd', on the site of the cottage where he was born in 1770.*

'Scott's View' (below), *over the Eildon Hills near Melrose, is said to have been a favourite of the novelist.*

Hermitage Castle (left), *Roxburghshire, was a fortress of the Douglases, built in the 14th century but since restored. Mary, Queen of Scots, visited the castle in 1566 and, indeed, nearly died of a fever there.*

The neighbouring Border Forest (above), *the largest man-made forest in Europe, extends deep into England.*

St Mary's Loch (above), *Selkirk, is one of the most beautiful in the Lowlands. The Ettrick Shepherd grazed his flocks in the nearby hills, and Scott brought it into 'Marmion'.*

The Palace of Falkland (right), *Fife, one of the Royal Burghs, was a favourite of the Scottish Court: James V, Mary, Queen of Scots, Charles I and Charles II all visited it. Typically Cromwell is blamed for having burnt the East Wing in 1654.*

Although this book is mainly concerned with the Scottish countryside, it is hard to resist including a page or two on Edinburgh. Much less spoilt by the 20th-century philistine than other capital cities, it has an air of being nicely poised between order and disorder, sedateness and bustle, the classical and the romantic. The Changing of the Guard at the Castle (top right) shows that regard for heritage that any city, with its roots deep in the past, allows itself. The view of Princes Street and the Castle from Calton Hill (bottom right) is an impressive panorama of a great city. From such setpieces it is only a step to the earthy huddle of the Royal Mile, where so many houses are packed together that there is hardly room between for the alleys and courtyards, such as White Horse Close (below).

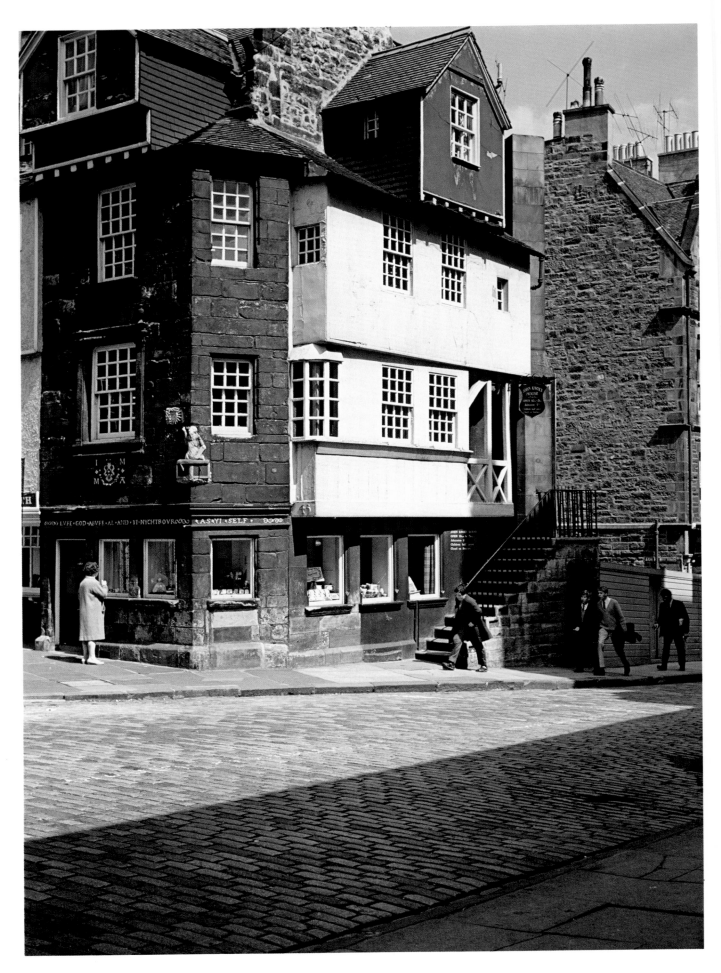

(Left) *John Knox's House, Edinburgh.*
Princes Street from Edinburgh Castle.

The beauties of Yarrow Vale, Selkirk, inspired Scott and Wordsworth, among others, while Yarrow Kirk contains relics of James Hogg, the Ettrick Shepherd. Yarrow Water (top right) *runs down the Vale from St Mary's Loch to Selkirk, and the cottage* (bottom right)*, with its well-kept garden, is typical of this Lowland country.*

(Below) *A picturesque lochan near Selkirk.*

The southeast coast has some curious rock formations. At St Abb's Head (top right) *the uptilting of the rocks, followed by marine erosion along the joints, has left these impressive stacks. Once smugglers made use of this heavily indented coast, with its caves, but now it is abandoned to the birds. Bass Rock* (bottom right), *a sudden upsurge of land just off the coast, is almost hidden by the gannets* (below).

Dunbar (below) *and Eyemouth* (left) *are both old east coast fishing ports where the wind blows cold off the North Sea and the women's thick knitted socks and sweaters are always welcomed.*

Culross, Fife, is another Royal Burgh, and the Palace (below) dates from a few years on either side of 1600. The pantiles are typical of Culross and also of Crail (bottom right), yet another Royal Burgh.

The impressive Leaderfoot railway viaduct (top right) over the Tweed, now disused, like so many others.

The River Esk, near Canonbie, Dumfriesshire.

There is a striking contrast between Highland farms and these Lowland ones, near New Abbey (left) and near Mainsriddle.

The Sark Toll Bar house (top right), *just inside the border with England, was one of several places (Gretna is the best-known) where runaway marriages were performed under Scots law.*

New Abbey (below), *in the Kirkcudbrightshire village* (bottom right) *of the same name, is also popularly known as Sweetheart Abbey. It was founded in 1273 by a lady with the rather forbidding name of Devorgilla, who also endowed Balliol College, Oxford. She was buried at her death, with the heart of her husband, before the High Altar, from which the Abbey gained the name of 'Dulce Cor' or Sweetheart.*

At Ruthwell, Dumfriesshire, is preserved a remarkable late 7th-century stone cross (right). The figure carving is of such quality as to point to a link with Classical sculpture, doubtless through Northumbria, which after the Synod of Whitby (664) adopted the practices of the Roman Church and ended the supremacy there of the independent Celtic Church.

Figure carving of well over a millennium later can be seen in the garden of Souter Johnnie's cottage (below), at Kirkoswald, Ayrshire. They represent some of Burns's most famous characters, with the landlord and his wife flanking Tam o' Shanter and Souter Johnnie himself.

Caerlaverock Castle, Dumfriesshire, a Maxwell
fortress, is unusual in having a triangular enclosure.
The Covenanters besieged it for three months in 1640.

Strange rocky outcrops at Ross Point,
Kirkcudbrightshire.

*A heathery glen in the Lowther Hills,
Dumfriesshire.*

Horses still find a place on the farm in Kirkcudbrightshire, whether for harrowing or in forestry in the Kirroughtree Forest, where the steep terrain makes tractors unsuitable.

Culzean Castle, Ayrshire, designed by Robert Adam, dates from 1777. General Eisenhower was presented with a flat here after the Second World War as a residence in Scotland.

Near Castle Douglas, Kirkcudbrightshire, the gardens of Threave House (above) are used by the National Trust for Scotland as its School of Gardening.

The Burns statue (top) in Dumfries, where the poet is buried.

The Grey Mare's Tail waterfall (bottom right),
near Birkhill, Dumfriesshire, is 200ft high.

At Ross Point (below), *Kirkcudbrightshire, the tilted
and cleaved Silurian rocks, covered with lichen and
scoured by the tides, make a striking foreshore, while
Kirkcudbright Bay at low tide* (top right) *provides
its own blend of colours from seaweed, rock and water.*

The Nith Estuary, near Glen Caple, Dumfriesshire.

Acknowledgments

The photographers were responsible for the illustrations as follows:

W. F. Davidson: pages 16, 17, 20 bottom, 26, 27, 28, 29, 36 bottom, 38, 42, 43, 44, 47, 50, 51, 52, 54 bottom, 57, 59, 63, 66, 67, 74, 75, 77, 80, 81, 84, 85, 86, 87, 88, 89, 90-91, 92, 93, 94, 95, 96, 97, 98, 99, 100, 101, 102, 103, 105 top, 107, 108, 109, 110-111, 112, 113, 114, 115, 116, 117, 118, 119, 120, 121, 122, 123, 124, 125, 126-127

R. Thomlinson: frontispiece and pages 8, 12-13, 14, 15, 18, 19, 20 top, 21, 22, 23, 24, 25, 30, 31, 32, 33, 34-35, 36 top, 37, 39, 40, 41, 45, 46, 48-49, 53, 54 top, 55, 56, 58, 60-61, 62, 64-65, 68-69, 70, 71, 72, 73, 76, 78, 79, 82-83, 104, 105 bottom, 106